CLIENTS

How to Land Clients and Build Long-Lasting Relationships

~ Bob Abramson ~

Download The FREE Companion Course For This Book:

http://www.bobabramson.com/companion-course

WOW YOUR CLIENTS: How to Land Clients and Build Long-Lasting Relationships Copyright 2016 by Bob Abramson LLC. All rights reserved.
ISBN-13: 978-1540595225
ISBN-10: 1540595226

Published by Bob Abramson LLC.
Published in the United States of America
Printed by CreateSpace (createspace.com)

No part of this book may be reproduced in any form or by any means electronically or otherwise, unless permission has been granted by the author, with the exception of brief excerpts for review purposes.

This book may not be re-sold or given away to other people. If you would like to share this book with another person, please purchase an additional copy for each recipient. Thank you for respecting the work of this author and for not violating any copyright laws.

Cover creation by Kathleen Ruhl of
http://www.kathleenruhl-artist.weebly.com

Editing and formatting courtesy of Lorraine Reguly from https://wordingwell.com/.

Contents

Introduction: Coveted 1

Chapter 1: The Launching Pad – How Do You Get Off the Ground Floor and Find Clients? 15

Chapter 2: The Key to Networking – Get Over Yourself! 23

Chapter 3: Have You Got the Look? 29

Chapter 4: The Art of Working a Conference .. 35

Chapter 5: Marinate 43

Chapter 6: Follow-Up is Critical 49

Chapter 7: Go for Broke! 53

Chapter 8: Persistence Will Pay Off 61

Chapter 9: How to Generate Clients through Speaking 67

Chapter 10: Dazzle, and Earn Repeat Business and Referrals 73

Chapter 11: Your 90-Day Action Plan 81

Chapter 12: Author's Note + Book Recommendations 85

Chapter 13: About the Author 87

Chapter 14: Book Bob to Speak at Your Next Event 89

Chapter 15: Free Bonuses 91

"Everyone wants to live on top of the mountain, but all the happiness and growth occurs while you're climbing it."

— Andy Rooney

Introduction: Coveted

At 3 a.m., ten guys pulled me out of bed.

They grabbed my arms and legs, picked me up, then carried me out of the room, down the hallway, down the stairs, out the front door, and tossed me into a van.

Only then, did I realize for the first time that I was pledging a fraternity.

It was a cold Friday morning in January 1992. I was in the second semester of my freshman year at the University of Michigan.

I always wanted to be in a fraternity, ever since I saw John Belushi in "Animal House," or Booger and Takashi in "Revenge of The Nerds."

My brother, Joel, is four years older than me, and was part of a fraternity at our rival school, Michigan State. While I was in high school, he would occasionally bring me up for the weekend.

I got my first taste of fraternity life. Wild parties. Hot girls.

Wow! When can I start college?

Now, it was my turn.

I specifically picked this fraternity in the rush process because I liked the brothers, and they did not haze their pledges.

The next ninety days of my pledge term were a blur. When I wasn't in class or studying, I was hanging out at the fraternity house... and drinking. Or we were going to parties, meeting girls... and drinking.

I never woke up with so many nasty hangovers in my whole life.

Each of the pledges were assigned a big brother in the fraternity house. I happened to get the one who truly wasn't a big brother... because he was never there. He was missing in action.

It got to the point where I complained to my pledge-master. He agreed, secured a new big brother, and life moved on.

Still, I was truly enjoying the bond that was being fostered between me and my fellow pledges. It was something I had longed for, considering that I went to two different high schools in Michigan: Cranbrook, and West Bloomfield.

I was never the star athlete, or the most popular kid. I struggled to find my place.

The fraternity house felt like home.

With my freshman year winding down, I had to figure out where I was going to live during the next year. The fraternity took care of that dilemma – they made all the pledges sign leases to live in the fraternity house the following year.

With two weeks to go in the semester, I finally reached Initiation Day. I was excited about joining the brotherhood. Yet, I was also nervous, because initiations are very hush-hush in fraternities. You have no idea what to expect.

Do they dunk you in some sacred bath? Do they make you eat some weird food? Do you finally get to learn the secret handshake?

I put on the only suit that I owned – which, at age 19, was code for sport coat, khaki pants, white shirt, red tie – and made my way over to the fraternity house, a walk I had completed hundreds of times that semester. As I opened up the giant front doors, standing before me was my pledge-master, the guy who had guided me the previous three months.

Without saying a word, he immediately whisked me off to a side room.

Thirteen of my pledge brothers and I huddled together in this tiny room. We waited there for what seemed like an eternity… until I heard, "Abramson, let's go!"

When your last name starts with "A," you are used to going first. It has been that way ever since I was a little kid.

I guess I was going to be the guinea pig.

They led me out to the main room of the fraternity house, which had these spectacular high ceilings, and beautiful oak everywhere you looked. Yet the room still exhibited that musty smell of beer and sex from the night before.

It wasn't until they sat me down at a long table that I realized I was perched up really high, like a judge in a courtroom, looking straight down.

The main floor of the house was dimly lit, but I could clearly see forty-five fraternity brothers, all staring straight up at me.

It was *intimidating*.

One by one, some of the fraternity brothers started firing questions at me.

"Bob, how come you didn't get along with your big brother? What was going on there?"

Before I got a chance to answer, another brother stood up, and said, "Bob, how come we didn't see you at the fraternity house for four days? Where were you?"

My head was spinning. I wondered, "*Where was this all coming from? When do we get to the fun ceremonies?*"

Then the final shot rang from another brother. "Bob, you're done."

"What do you mean, done?"

He said, "You are done. Forever. Get out of here. Now!"

I was numb. Leveled. Absolutely humiliated.

I got up, and bolted out of that fraternity house for the last time in my life.

It is about a mile walk from the fraternity house to my dorm room in South Quad. That day, it felt like 26.2 miles. I never cried so hard in my whole life. I was crying harder than it was raining outside.

What now?

What do I tell my parents? My friends?

They all thought I was going to be welcomed into this fraternity. Yet, here I was, trudging home in the rain, while my thirteen pledge brothers were about to be initiated.

I kept asking myself, "*What is wrong with me? Why didn't they like me?*"

Did I just get blackballed?

With my clothes drenched, I slammed the door to my dorm room, tore up the lease into a million pieces, got into bed, and curled up into a fetal position for hours.

To this day, I still don't know what I did wrong. I thought I did everything that I was supposed to do to get into that fraternity.

Maybe I should have never said something about my big brother. Perhaps I should have been at the house every single day.

During the entire ninety days I was pledging, nobody gave me any indication that I was doing anything improper. They led me down a path to believe that when I stood before them, I was going to join the brotherhood.

In reality, I got completely duped.

Tossed, like a piece of garbage.

They left me high and dry, with nowhere to live for the next year.

My 19-year-old spirit was crushed.

The ironic thing was, I specifically picked this fraternity because they did not haze their pledges. Yet, what ended up happening to me was far worse than any good-natured hazing.

When you are down in the dumps, or lying in the ditch, and all you can think about is how you got there, you need a diversion. You need to get your mind on something else.

That's what I did.

I decided right then and there, that from here on in – no matter what I did, or where I went – I was going to become indispensable. Coveted. To the point where people would be asking *me* to join their inner circles.

I went back for my sophomore year, and lived with three guys I did not know. One of them was in a band. I changed my major to communications, and dove into writing.

Just over two years later, on July 1, 1994, my byline appeared on the front page of USA Today's sports section, the nation's largest newspaper.

I was 21 years old.

I went on to become an award-winning professional sportswriter for seven years. I was voted the top investigative sports reporter in the state of Ohio for my newspaper division by the Associated Press.

In 1997, I landed my dream job, covering University of Michigan athletics. In my first season covering Michigan football, they won the national championship. I co-authored a book on their championship run, which sold 15,000 copies.

I was fortunate to interview a variety of athletes during my seven-year career, including Tom Brady, Earl Campbell, Martina Navratilova, Grant Hill, Mia Hamm, and Ernie Harwell.

By 2002, I sensed that newspapers were starting to die out across the country. The internet was destroying subscriptions, and the cost of printing paper was through the roof.

I knew I had to make a change. I didn't want to become extinct.

My plan was to go to graduate school for Public Relations. One morning, I met my father for breakfast to convey this news.

Rather than embrace my idea, my father provided me with an alternate suggestion: become a lawyer. He told me that, with a law degree, I would never be unemployed, could work in different fields, and earn a quality living. (I was making $35,000 annually, after seven years as a sportswriter.)

I signed up for a Kaplan course the next day to prepare to get into law school. It was inarguably the best piece of advice my father ever gave me.

I took the LSAT in June 2002, got married in July 2002 to my dynamite wife, Alyson, was accepted to law school upon returning from my honeymoon, quit my job, and began going to law school full-time in August 2002.

In 2005, I graduated, and passed the bar. During job interviews, most law partners routinely asked me the same question: "Why in the world would you leave a job covering University of Michigan football to be a *lawyer*?"

A valid question.

The truth is, the job wasn't as glorious as it seemed to an outsider. Don't get me wrong – being a sportswriter is an exciting profession. The downside is long hours, lots of travel, and lousy pay. Your life is ruled by sports schedules. That is no way to live.

I used to go to bed at 3 a.m. and get up at 11 a.m. By the time I woke up, I felt like I was missing out on great things in the world.

Today, I love getting up at 5 a.m.

I have been a practicing lawyer for over a decade. I made equity partner in just five years, and have brought in over a million dollars of business to my law firm.

It turns out, that being blackballed – for as much as it sucked -- was the best thing that ever happened to me.

I decided to write this book not for payback, *but to give back*. Through all my trials and tribulations, it dawned on

me that very few business professionals and budding entrepreneurs actually understand how and/or possess the ability to bring in business and build long-term relationships with clients.

No one teaches you those skills in graduate school. You show up in your job, and are simply expected to generate revenue out of thin air.

Whether you want to bring in business and have no idea where to start, or have been plugging away and are stuck in a rut, I wrote this book to show you the path, and light a fire under you. I did it to help you raise your game, and build the career you have always desired.

Climbing the mountain won't be easy. You will endure your share of rejection. Could it be any worse than what I went through with my fraternity? Probably not. Through those experiences, you learn to develop a tough exterior, gain an understanding of what works with clients, and what doesn't work.

No matter what your situation, there are three critical steps to developing a business and creating long-lasting relationships:

(1) Marinate.
(2) Go for broke.
(3) Dazzle.

No, you won't be marinating steaks. When I say "marinate," I mean that you have to be patient. It takes time to get someone's business. You have to develop and foster a personal relationship long before business comes your way. If you don't do this, you will never get to steps two and three.

"Go for broke" is the step where people usually tense up. It is the moment of truth. The time to ask for someone's business. I will walk you through the step of how to overcome your fears, and pitch in such a way that they have no choice but to say yes!

The term "dazzle" speaks for itself. Once you get the client, I will show you unique methods to not only garner repeat business, but impress your client so much that they brag to everyone they know about you.

This is the foundation for securing your ideal client, or expanding your relationship with your current clients.

Are you ready to wow your clients and light a fire in your business?

Before you head off to the next chapter, print out and fill out your business self-assessment plan at www.bobabramson.com/companion-course.

This will allow you to step back, figure out where you are, where you go want to, and lay out your roadmap for success

Chapter 1: The Launching Pad – How Do You Get Off the Ground Floor and Find Clients?

"To the degree we're not living our dreams, our comfort zone has more control of us than we have over ourselves." --- Peter McWilliams

In 2010, I didn't know a damn thing about how to bring in business to my law firm.

Law school prepared me to think like a lawyer. Looking back, I realize there were *zero* classes specifically tailored to finding clients.

The fact is, what colleges and graduate schools *don't do* is teach people how to connect, cultivate, develop, acquire and keep clients.

I was clueless where to even *start*.

Who do you call?

That's what happens when you are a typical associate defense lawyer, shielded from clients as if they have an electronic force field surrounding them. The partners handle the day-to-day client communication and the business logistics; the associates work up the files.

Your life is ruled and measured by one thing: billable hours. Daily, monthly, and yearly requirements.

Every day you come into work, the requirement must be met, or exceeded. The pressure is constant, but understandable. The more hours a law firm bills, the more the bottom line (revenue) increases.

By this point, I was completely tapped out. My brain had been oversaturated, and reached the point of maximum billable capacity. There are only so many hours you can bill in a day. Unfortunately, when your earning power is based solely on your billable hours output, you hit a ceiling.

My law career reached a crossroad: I could either be content in my position, knowing I was my boss' right-hand man, and remain status quo; or I could switch gears, separate myself from the pack, and become a self-made client generator.

I chose to dive in, head first, to the unknown world of business development.

Like any other profession, the best way to learn something is to seek out and latch on to people who excel and are THE BEST in the areas where you ultimately want to thrive.

Medical residents watch brilliant surgeons in action to see how they perform complex brain surgeries. Those with freshly-minted broker's licenses follow around the savvy realtor to witness how to perfectly land a new listing. Young bucks tag alongside the veteran financial advisor to bear witness to him/her delicately balancing a couple's financial concerns involving their entire life savings.

Everyone needs to gain real-life work experience and expertise. It is the time-tested ritual of growth, the passing of the torch.

The reality is, very few souls actually desire to be business producers. Most avoid it like the plague. They come up with an endless string of excuses, routinely claiming it is not their forte, that their schedule is too packed to squeeze something else in, or they are not fond of the idea of traveling. They are mired in complacency, and do not want to disrupt their pre-packaged days.

In the end, who is going to be more attractive, coveted, and rise up quicker in their profession: the behind-the-desk biller, or the person with the book of business?

It's a no-brainer.

If this is where you want to go, in order to begin that quest, let your intentions be known. Put it out there to the world. Advise your superiors of your willingness and desire to add to the company's bottom line.

Depending on where you work, don't be surprised if you feel the weight of resistance. Some bosses may be stuck in that old-school, top-down, mentality. They purposely discourage others from developing business, so they can maintain their Kung Fu grip on that arena. They are so anal that they don't want anyone invading their territory. The pie is theirs. *How dare anyone try to take a piece!*

If this is where you work... think about a new home. Seriously. You do not want to find this out five years into your career.

Other companies may be intrigued and receptive to the idea of taking you under their wing. You know why? Because 90 percent of business is usually brought in by a select few. If one of their client generators leaves – or dies – a lot of dollars may suddenly evaporate. Companies need diversification, both in their clientele, and in those who can bring in the clients. These companies know that it is important to invest time and development with younger and newer talent – namely, YOU.

Let these business developer gurus be your Jedi masters. Soak up their knowledge like a sponge. Be assertive. Ask them if you can tag along to conferences, meetings, and sales pitches to see how they magically win clients over. There is nothing quite like watching a master at work. Then, when it is your turn to shine, you can follow their time-tested formulas and execute the closing.

When I first made my intentions known to become the next business generator, it was met with open arms. I went on client trips with each of the four named partners in my firm (at the time), all terrific business developers in their own right. Each of them had their own unique style.

I sat back, listened intently, took copious notes, watched how they operated, and plucked great ideas from each one of them. Then I developed my own shtick, brought in numerous clients from the ground up, and evolved into an elite business producer.

There is nothing quite like having great mentors to show you the way. They are such rare finds that when you do happen to stumble upon them, it's as if you received a gift from the Gods. Henry David Thoreau, author of "Walden," was mentored by Ralph Waldo Emerson. Detroit Free Press newspaper columnist Mitch Albom was so thankful for what he learned from Morrie Schwartz, his former professor at Brandeis University, that he penned a book called *Tuesdays with Morrie*. Two-time Academy Award winner Denzel Washington evolved into a dynamite actor because actor Sydney Portier showed him the way.

If you are blessed enough to work at a place that has some business all-stars in the upper ranks, and supports the idea of the ambitious up-and-comers learning the trade, capitalize on the situation. Don't become so entrenched or comfortable in your career that you sit back and let this opportunity slip past you.

ACTIONABLE TIPS

The fact is, you are never too busy to pencil in time to develop your business. Everyone's calendars are filled with meetings, conference calls, and assignments. Why not do the same thing by setting aside and blocking out an allotted chunk of time each day to concentrate on obtaining clients?

Start out small. Maybe make one business call per day. Or work your way up to setting aside an hour per day. Or get out of the office for half a day to visit a few potential clients.

Sure, this may throw off your routine, or force you to shift the way you operate. Maybe you will have to hit the road, and be away from your family for a few days at a time. Perhaps you will have to work some extra hours on the weekend.

But if you do these things, trust me, your business will take off like a rocket!

In order to begin your transformation, print out your 25 tips to light a fire in your business --- get the tips at www.bobabramson.com/companion-course.

Then hang it up on your bathroom mirror, so it will greet you every morning, and remind you what you need to do to WOW your clients. It takes 66 days to form a new, long-lasting habit. Get started today!

Chapter 2: The Key to Networking – Get Over Yourself!

"The mark of a good conversationalist is not that you can talk a lot. The mark is that you can get others to talk a lot. Thus, good schmoozer's are good listeners, not good talkers." --- Guy Kawasaki

I don't think I have ever met a single person who does not like to talk about themselves. We all do. It's part of our DNA.

Everybody wants to share how great they are, what an amazing job they just did, or how they are raking in money. Perhaps they want to tell you how generous they are with the world, or how their contribution to mankind is life-changing.

I have seen people post on Facebook how they were at a store, and decided out of the goodness of their heart to start offering $100 bills to pay for the family waiting in line in front of them. Or they bought coffees for everyone in line behind them at Starbucks.

They are paying it forward. They get 122 comments, and 7,673 likes on their

Facebook page. They feel even better about themselves.

There is a plaintiff's lawyer in Detroit who regularly advertises on television. He talks about the great settlements he gets for his clients. He has his wife and sister vouch for him. He has even popped up on a reality television show.

One day, I saw a different type of ad from him. He told the story of how he gave over half a million dollars to fund inner-city kids with school supplies. It was jaw-dropping and impressive – even to a defense lawyer like me!

We all love to hear about these stories. They warm our hearts. It is a nice break from the assault of the sad news stories we see every night on television. Terrorism. Murder. Indictments of federal officials. It is no wonder that NBC Nightly News now closes their nightly broadcast with an uplifting story that is bound to get to you to break out the tissues.

Don't get me wrong – these are all incredibly nice gestures. But YOU don't need to send out your own press releases, and broadcast it to the world.

Your reward is the internal satisfaction you felt at that moment after seeing the reaction on the faces of that family. Could there be anything better in life than buying Christmas gifts for kids who have never been able to afford them, or assisting a mother who is mustering up every last cent to feed her family?

How good did that moment feel? It is indescribable.

I don't go around telling people, "Hey, I just donated money to the University of Michigan Children's Hospital. Aren't you impressed?"

During a cold Michigan winter day, I was walking back from a court appearance to my car. A homeless man approached me. He asked me for money. I asked him, "Why do you need it?" He told me he was a tradesman who fell on rough times and got laid off. I handed him $20. I had no idea whether he was going to buy food, smokes, alcohol, or drugs. My hunch was cigarettes.

I felt conflicted. Did I just do the right thing, or contribute to his habit?

Either way, I felt better. I did a good deed, and felt warm and fuzzy inside. But I didn't go home and tell my wife – or anyone else. Bragging is not what philanthropists do. You won't see Warren Buffett, Bill Gates, or Mark Zuckerberg advertising their latest humanitarian efforts. Instead, they keep the secret to themselves.

If word gets out, and someone else wants to share what you did, so be it. Let them promote your efforts. It is far more powerful to hear from the people whose lives you have impacted than your own self-promotion.

Take Jalen Rose, for example. He was the trash-talking point guard of the "Fab Five," leading University of Michigan basketball to back-to-back NCAA final appearances. He went on to play 13 years in the NBA. Then he transitioned to become the lead studio NBA host for ESPN. That's quite a career!

For all his accomplishments, what is inarguably his greatest contribution and lasting legacy is the Jalen Rose Leadership

Academy. This is an open-enrollment, charter high school he co-founded in Detroit. When the first seniors graduated in 2015, you should have heard the stories that were told by the very people he deeply impacted. They were awesome!

ACTIONABLE TIPS

If you want to thrive in the business world, lose your ego at the door. Life does not revolve around you.

Keep this in mind the next time you are at a networking event.

Here's a challenge for you: When you meet someone new, try not to talk about yourself for the first five minutes.

It's tough.

As a former journalist, I was always fascinated to learn about other people's lives. Where they came from, where they are going, and the struggles they endured along the way.

When you meet people, pretend you are a journalist who has to write a short story on the person you are just

meeting. Follow the journalist credo: Who, What, When, Where, Why, and How.

This philosophy is no different than the one I used to utilize when I dated. On that first date, I would ask the girl a lot of questions because I was curious to figure out whether or not we were the right match for each other. Inevitably, after 45 minutes, the girl would say, "Wait a minute… I don't know anything about *you* yet."

Precisely.

The thing is, whether you are dating or networking, you don't need to volunteer and spit out how wonderful you are. That will eventually come to the forefront.

When you focus on finding out on what makes that other person tick, and how you can help them in their business or career, you are then in the beginning stages of forming a mutual, long-term, long-lasting business relationship.

Chapter 3: Have You Got the Look?

"Image is everything." --- Andre Agassi

I was in La Jolla, California, one of the most beautiful places in the world. The rock formations are incredible. The seals are a sight to behold. There are few better places to watch a sunset than on the outdoor deck of George's restaurant with a glass of wine in hand.

Yet, I was stuck inside an auditorium. I sat all day long, waiting to give my speech at 6:30 p.m.

I knew some of the people in the audience. They were in a mastermind group with me. We had either spent a weekend training together or gone out to dinner.

I don't know if these four women planned their assault, but it sure felt that way. At different points of the day, each of them came up to me, and started to give me fashion advice:

"Bob, when you were here yesterday, it looked like you had on 'Mom' jeans. Throw those out!"

"Bob, you need to wear clothes that fit your body!"

"Bob, you have an athletic build, but you would never know it by the clothes you wear."

"Bob, you need to find a personal shopper."

Just before I was about to go onstage, I was standing backstage with Tim Adams, who is the personal trainer for the singer Usher. (www.coachtimadams.com) Tim was working with Bo Eason while Bo was breaking from his Personal Story Power Event.

I had on a blue suit, blue shirt, no tie, and brown shoes. Tim stops working on Bo… and he tells me to discard the jacket. It is too big.

Then he literally starts stuffing my shirt tightly into my pants to make it fit better and sends me off on stage.

It was my fashion awakening.

The day after I came home from La Jolla, I told my wife Alyson about what had transpired. She reminded me that she had been telling me for two years that my clothes were too big, and I did not listen to her.

When your wife tells you something, it is one thing. When five other people are brutally honest with you, the message rings home.

I don't know why I wore the clothes I did. I certainly never intended to hide my build. I am in good shape. They just felt comfortable to wear. Plus, I had lost 17 pounds over a two-year period, so they were even bigger than when I first bought them! I was practically swimming in those clothes.

I did not realize the sloppy image I was projecting.

The week after I returned home, we called up Nordstorm, and lined up an appointment with a personal shopper. There is a first time for everything. It was a weird experience to wear clothes that were tighter and actually conformed to my body.

I had never bought a $200 pair of jeans in my life… until that day.

I will never wear baggy clothes again (except sweatpants, at home).

After that day, people started coming up to me, and saying, "I can't put my finger on it, but there is something different about you."

Yes, clothes do make the man.

ACTIONABLE TIPS

When it comes to business, it is all about "the look." Is there anything more magnetic than a woman in a dynamite outfit, or a man in a sharp, tailored three-piece suit? It stops us in our tracks.

The fact is – like it or not – people judge you on how you look. What you are wearing the first time you meet them could be the difference as to whether or not they ultimately become your client.

When you are speaking on stage, if you want to be taken seriously, don't go to the discount suit store. It can detract from what is otherwise a dynamite presentation. If you have ever watched the show Millionaire

Listing, look how well those guys dress. It is no wonder they are landing the listings of the rich and famous!

I am not saying to empty the closet and overhaul your whole wardrobe tomorrow. Go look in your closet tonight, and pull out your business clothes. Decide which ones absolutely need to be discarded.

Buy slim-fitting clothes that accentuate your body. Theory.com sells terrific suits for men, and the tight pants even stretch.

Make your wardrobe changes slowly, and watch how your business transforms in the process.

Should you be out selling and networking before you learn how to dress?

"If you don't build your dream, someone else will hire you to help them build theirs."

— Dhirubhai Ambani, founder, Reliance Industries

Chapter 4: The Art of Working a Conference

"Preparation for life is so important. Luck is what happens when preparedness meets opportunity. Opportunity is all around us. Are you prepared?" --- *Earl Nightingale*

There are 4 phases involved when working a conference.

Phase 1: SCOUTING

Most people just show up to a conference, walk without direction, and hope to get business. The seasoned business developer plans his networking strategy well in advance.

Before arriving on the conference turf, it is critical to call up the organizer and secure the coveted list of attendees. This is where the reconnaissance mission begins.

Comb the list, one-by-one, to determine existing and potential clients. Google everybody. Find out their hobbies, school affiliations, organizations they are a part of, and make notes next to their names. Those will come in handy

when it comes to making that personal connection during that chance meeting.

Also, for people that you truly want to target, print out a copy of their headshot so you have a better opportunity of recognizing them when you get there. It beats squinting when trying to read their nametags.

Boxing legend Muhammad Ali once said, "The fight is won or lost far away from witnesses – behind the lines, in the gym, and out there on the road, long before I dance under those lights."

Phase 2: FIVE HOURS OF GUARANTEED NETWORKING

Most conferences include "extra" activities that you can sign up for. These are great ways to connect with others.

Networking during these activities is a MUST!

Getting to know others in a different atmosphere will help you to form relationships on a different level, which

you can then leverage when turning these people into your clients.

If golf is part of the conference, sign up to be put in a foursome, no matter what your skill level is. It is okay... most people suck at golf!

As Hall of Fame baseball player Hank Aaron once said, "It took me seventeen years to get three thousand hits in baseball. It took one afternoon on the golf course."

If you can't even make contact with the ball off the tee, perhaps a couple of pre-conference lessons are in order. Remember this: You just have to be serviceable on the course. This is because the format will likely be "best ball," meaning the foursome just plays the best shot each time.

If possible, ask the organizer to be paired with the "decision-makers" at a company you are targeting. No matter how poor your putting skills are, when you are stuck together in a golf cart for five hours, there is no better way to get to know someone. There is a reason so many deals are made in that time frame!

Just make sure you don't cheat, or snap your pitching wedge in two. Your actions on the golf course will speak volumes about your character.

Phase 3: REMEMBERING THAT TIME IS OF THE ESSENCE

Check out the schedule of events ahead of time. This is particularly important for first-time attendees. Otherwise, the conference is going to be a blur.

A sample conference may consist of:

Breakfast

Speakers

Keynote lunches

More Speakers

Cocktail Networking

Extravagant Dinners

After parties

And more…

Conferences are exhausting. You will likely be getting only three or four hours of sleep each night, so try to chart out your course of attack, remember to pace yourself, reserve dinner with clients ahead of time (if possible), and be ready to go *on time*.

Phase 4: GAME TIME

Kobe Bryant's work ethic is legendary. In the 2008 Olympics, Coach Jim Boeheim referred to him as the hardest-working player he had ever been around. According to Boeheim, he would work out before practice, he practiced harder than any of his teammates, and then he would work out again after practice.

You should follow his lead at a conference.

ACTIONABLE TIPS

Here are 7 tips to help you be a success at a conference.

Right before you head in for the first time, use this little trick:

1: Put your business cards in your right pocket with a pen; and place the business cards people give you in your left pocket.

This way, the two will never get commingled.

2: Arrive early, and stay until the end.

As the first one there, you possess the unique opportunity to meet more people than anyone else. Introduce yourself to everyone… even if they look weird.

3: Although we all love to talk about ourselves, keep the bragging to a minimum.

It is far more important to find out what other people do, and what makes them tick. (Recall the 5 Ws and the H from Chapter 2!)

Even if you think their business has no connection to yours, and you are ready to prematurely terminate the conversation, *you never know who they know.*

***That* person may become your next client down the road.**

You are going to meet hundreds of people, and your brain is not built to remember everyone's story. So use the next tip to remedy this!

4: As you conclude each conversation, collect a business card, and before moving on to the next person, write "reminder" notes on the back of that card.

For example: big University of Michigan football fan; has two kids; hates golfing, loves sushi, worked with (fill in the name of the person), enjoys singing.

Otherwise, you are going to get back from that conference, look at the card, scratch your head, and say, "Who was that?"

These reminders will serve you well in the future. You'll be able to connect with that person again if you bond over a common interest (or dislike), or if you say something memorable.

5: Be constantly on the move. After each speaker, shift to a different seat, so you can be exposed to other people.

Eventually, you will get to the best part... the cocktail networking hour. Just be sure to watch your alcohol intake. The night is young!

6: Look for additional ways to network.

Some conferences have what are known as "dine-arounds," meaning you can sign up for dinner at various locations with random people (which usually includes a three-course meal with unlimited wine). Or, if you are alone, and the conference does not offer this feature, do not be shy! Ask people seated around you if they want to join you for dinner.

These are the true opportunities to get to know people. Even if you are tired, seize the moment. Because once people go back to their offices, you are lucky if they will take your phone call or respond to your email.

7: Become a speaker at the next event.

Before you exit the conference, find out who is in charge of putting together the speakers for the next event. Volunteer to sign up.

Once you are on that stage the following year, and give a memorable performance, your credibility rises ten-fold.

Chapter 5: Marinate

"The key to this business is personal relationships." --- Dickey Fox, character from "Jerry Maguire"

In early 2007, before the economy went in the tank, my wife came to me with an idea.

"I think we should buy a rental property."

Naturally, I was hesitant. Renting out houses is a risky proposition.

Tenants are wild cards. They can trash your home, move out in the middle of the night, and leave you high and dry, with an unrented place for months and a second mortgage that could cripple you.

I didn't know the first thing about owning a rental property. But I did my due diligence, ran the numbers, and concluded that we could make it work.

The problem was, we had no idea who would be the best-suited realtor to advise us, and help us find the right property. So we drove up and down our neighborhood, nearby subdivisions, and compiled a list of names.

We left messages for 17 realtors. *One* called us back. Paul Mruk.

Turns out, that realtor owned approximately a dozen rental properties. He told us about his personal experiences – both good and bad – to provide us with keen insights into what we could be facing down the road.

Yet he also spent a lot of time asking questions. He found out who I was, what I did for a living, and where I wanted to go in life. (www.paulmruk.com)

I guess he truly listened, because a few months later, he introduced me to his neighbor, Mark Dolin, who happened to be the managing partner of a law firm.

Since 2007, that neighbor and I have been working together as partners in the same law firm.

Yes, I did eventually purchase that rental property.

But this isn't about endorsing my real estate agent … although I am forever indebted to him. It is to stress that business is about far more than *just the sale*.

Many people are able to develop the skill set to become professionals such as realtors, financial advisors, or lawyers. Remarkably, few are trained on how to open up their own practice, or to develop clients.

How do you persuade people to list or sell their home with you?

How do you persuade someone that you are the right person to handle their precious personal finances?

How do you persuade someone that you are the right lawyer to defend their case?

ACTIONABLE TIPS

You may have developed an expertise in your field, but the true secret is to figure out how to make that personal connection with that prospective client, and foster that relationship to make it a long-lasting one.

There's no secret sauce, or magic formula.

Find out where they are from, where they went to school, the sports teams they root for, the ages of their children, and their hobbies outside of work. The key is to probe, until you eventually find a common ground. This is what I spent years perfecting while conducting interviews with thousands of athletes, who are not always willing to share the inner details of their personal lives.

For example, if you and your prospect are from the same state, or attended the same college, you have an immediate connection. Spend more time listening, and less time talking about yourself.

I can't stress this enough.

Don't worry … you will have plenty of opportunities to discuss potential business later on.

The first networking conference I ever attended was in downtown Chicago. As I have come to discover, they always kick these things off with the infamous cocktail reception hour.

I spotted this guy standing at a table by himself, with a drink in his hand. We talked for 20 minutes, and none of it had to do with business. I wasn't pushing my business card in his face.

The conversation touched upon Philadelphia, football, and family. This is inarguably the most crucial step in developing business. If you don't develop and foster the personal relationship, forget about that person ever becoming your client.

Turns out, he was the litigation manager for a major insurance company, and had a need for legal counsel in Indiana.

In under a half hours' time, I laid the foundation for securing my first client. Right place, right time.

If only getting everyone's business was that easy!

Looking back on it, one of the main reasons this happened is because I wasn't holed up in my office. I was in another state, putting myself out there.

Face these facts: If you don't first build and establish a personal relationship with someone, you will never get their business.

Would you give business to someone you just met?

"The minute you're satisfied with where you are, you aren't there anymore."

— Tony Gwynn

Chapter 6: Follow-Up is Critical

"Follow up the interview with a phone call. If Carrot Top can figure out how to use a phone, so can you." --- Tom Cole

Conferences are a terrific way to network and get business. You usually come back with an army of business cards, tons of great leads, and are pumped up about the prospect of some new clients.

Yet here is what I witness happen time and time again: you come back to your office, and get swept up in the hurricane of phone calls, meetings and deadlines. Before you know it, two weeks have vanished.

What have you done with all the great leads you collected?

Absolutely nothing.

This is so why so many people fall flat on their face when it comes to business development – they don't follow up on their hot leads. You have to re-connect in that first week, or trust me, it is never going to get done. Then you will have potentially blown some tremendous opportunities.

ACTIONABLE TIPS

Develop a tracking system for your leads. Every time I get off the phone with someone, before I do anything else, I put in my calendar the next time I am going to follow up.

If it is a hot lead, maybe a week or two. If not, perhaps I circle back every 3-6 months. Depending on your preferences, you can use Outlook, or another CRM (Customer Relationship Management) tool to keep you on task.

It is not just about following up. Be unique. Do something that will blow them away to get their attention. Go the extra mile.

Purchase a giant balloon with a nice to meet you message. Maybe a Costco cake if you found out the date of their birthday. People will appreciate that you are thoughtful, funny, and genuine.

If you truly want to set yourself apart, and become a client generator, you have to make a regular habit of immediately following up, and set yourself apart in the manner in which you do it.

To download a free follow-up tracker, go to www.bobabramson.com/companion-course.

Bob Abramson

"In the business world, the rearview mirror is always clearer than the windshield."

— Warren Buffett

Chapter 7: Go for Broke!

"I really wish I was less of a thinking man and more of a fool not afraid of rejection." -- - Billy Joel

Remember the trepidation you felt as a teenager when you first had to muster up the courage to ask a girl out?

You obsessed about that potential conversation all day. Maybe even weeks.

Should it be done face-to-face, at school? Over the phone? You strategized, schemed, and planned out to perfection precisely when and what were you going to say.

Yet, when that agonizing moment arrived, you began to sweat, started to fumble your words, froze up, and skated out of that conversation without asking the key question:

"Would you like to go on a date with me?"

Why does this happen? Because we are all terrified of rejection. It haunts us.

We would rather retreat to our safe zone than potentially experience a punch to the gut.

When it comes to asking for business, some people still act as if they are trapped inside a teenage boy's body. They can't seem to get the words out of their mouth.

Mission aborted. Opportunity blown.

You can't let fear win the day.

Woody Hayes, the former great Ohio State football coach, once said, "Paralyze resistance with persistence."

The real work begins well in advance of your first meeting. Scour the earth for every piece of possible information you can get your hands on over the internet about that potential client, and their company. Google them. Read the industry publications that they read. Know them inside and out.

Some companies put their core values right on the front page of their website. Check them out. See if they align with *your* company's core values.

Remember that this meeting is not about you. It is all about the client.

You have to reverse roles, step inside the client's brain, and ask yourself this: Why would they hire you over anyone else?

What makes you different?

Clients usually look for three things when deciding who to hire:

- (1) How is it going to save them costs?
- (2) How it is going to increase their profit margin?
- (3) How is it going to help them in the long run?

Metrics are huge these days. Numbers don't lie. People need to see with their own eyes and easily understand how you can help them.

Several years ago, my wife and I interviewed a number of financial advisors over a period of a few months. Ultimately, we settled on one because he came in incredibly prepared, stepped inside our brain, tapped into what we were looking for, and separated himself from the pack:

(1) He was not going to charge us any up-front or annual fees, like so many other financial companies did.
(2) He demonstrated to us a number of potential deductions that we were unaware of, and how they could lower our taxes and increase our profits.
(3) He showed us that, over the long-term, we would be able to save more money, pay for college tuition for both of our kids, and retire by age 60, which was one of our goals.

By the time he got done showing us these three things, it was a seamless transition to ask for our business. We were ready to sign up before the words came out of his mouth.

ACTIONABLE TIPS

If you truly want someone's business, use this three-step formula that I teach to my clients. Go in there with guns blazing. Blow the doors off.

Reverse the roles, put yourself in that other person's shoes, and demonstrate why you are their savior. Show them how you can provide a value that no one else has even tapped into.

Be unique, creative, and leave an unforgettable impression. Make a video. Dazzle them with cool charts and graphs.

Wouldn't your ears perk up if someone demonstrated to you they could make your job easier, help double your business, while simultaneously cutting costs?

When you are in the midst of your pitch, exhibit no fear. Be bold. Exude confidence, even if your insides are trembling.

There is simply never a right moment to go in for the kill. Believe me, this is hard. It is uncomfortable.

If a slight pause occurs in the conversation, and the opening is there, just ASK FOR IT!

Go for broke.

Here is an easy line I teach my clients to say that has a high conversion rate:

"So, are you ready to start working together?"

Then sit back … and wait. The pregnant pause is in effect. The onus has shifted.

The fact is, if you have followed my three-step formula, and tapped into what that client is seeking, they will want to work with you. Asking will be the easy part.

If you don't ask, you never know what their response may be. It may surprise you. Perhaps you caught them on just the right day, and they are open to your approach.

On the other hand, what is the worst thing they are going to say?

"No way."

"Let me think about it."

"Not right now, but perhaps when I am dead."

You have to learn to accept the fact that rejection may be in the cards. People have been through far worse experiences, and so have you.

Stephen King's first book, "Carrie," was rejected *thirty times* by publishers.

Abraham Lincoln lost eight elections before becoming President of the United States.

Mega pop/country star Taylor Swift was ostracized by the cliques in high school because she was fond of country music. It gave her the courage to walk up to record labels at 12 years old and jump into the music industry.

At 19 years old, Walt Disney was fired from his job at the Kansas City Star. He was told that he "lacked creativity." Walt was also turned down by 302 banks when he attempted to get funding for the first theme park. Thankfully, rejection didn't derail Mr. Disney.

Think those banks are kicking themselves today?

When you have dealt with devastating rejection in your personal life, getting turned down for business is like a walk in the park. It is never fun, but it pales in comparison to getting blackballed by your fraternity on the last day of a pledge term.

Sure, fear is always hovering over your right shoulder at that critical ask-for-the-business moment, whispering in your ear like an alter ego. But at least you are bold enough to walk the plank. Your insides are hardened.

No one can dispute this: your success rate is much higher if you actually dare to ask for their business.

What's holding you back?

Chapter 8: Persistence Will Pay Off

"The biggest hurdle is rejection. Any business you start, be ready for it. The difference between successful people and unsuccessful people is the successful people do all the things the unsuccessful people don't want to do. When 10 doors are slammed in your face, go to door 11 enthusiastically, with a smile on your face."

--- John Paul DeJoria

Frankly, I thought the idea was brilliant.

I had set up a meeting with the litigation manager from a small town insurance company to try and get their business for our law firm. He was a seasoned veteran, a conservative guy, who lived so close he could bike to work.

In the midst of attempting to dig up cool nuggets of info on this head honcho, I stumbled across something unique on the internet. He just published a book on Amazon. It was about him becoming a born-again Christian, and how many of the themes carried over to the law.

Not exactly a topic I could relate to. Nor could my boss. We were not of the same faith.

Near the end of the meeting, that manager started to blush when we mentioned his book. Still, he indicated he was pretty happy with the law firms he was currently utilizing, but would consider using our services. (This is a patented "rejection" response from most insurance companies.)

As soon as we got in the car, my boss suggested that we buy his book off Amazon, and send him a letter asking him to provide a signed copy to one of our named partners, who was the same faith.

The book was $14.95. This could be a great return on a small investment.

About a month later, I followed up with this manager to see where we stood. Since we had not received a signed copy of his book back, I wondered if he ever got it, so I asked him.

He replied: "What book?"…

"Hold on one second."

He put the phone down, but the speaker was still on. I could hear the ruffling of papers in the background.

I waited. Then I heard him speak again.

"Oh. Sorry. I never opened the package. I thought it was just more materials from your law firm."

All I could do was laugh. Hysterically.

My attitude has always been this: Even if I don't get your business today, you will eventually hire me. Whether it is six months, or three years down the road, the timing just has to be right.

In the meantime, what will distinguish you from your competitors is that you are relentless. Persistent. Act as if you are not going to give up until you beat cancer.

I am not advocating stalking. But it doesn't hurt to keep gently reminding your prospective client that you are hanging around their neighborhood.

Tom Izzo is a legendary basketball coach at Michigan State University. Before that, he was an assistant coach at Northern University. For two straight years, Izzo came down to Lansing and requested to join Jud Heathcote's coaching staff. Heathcote did not have any openings.

When Izzo came down for the third straight year, Heathcote had an opening as a graduate assistant. He hired him because he figured anyone who was that persistent would likely be a good hire.

ACTIONABLE TIPS

So how do you stay in that potential prospect's brain without becoming a pest? Let them know what you are doing, and get personal with them.

When you go to pick up the mail at home, if there is a pile of bills, and a card sent personally to you, I can virtually guarantee you are going to open up that card first. Why? Because it rarely happens anymore. It makes you feel warm and fuzzy inside.

We live in an age of lightning correspondence. Email and texts provide us instant feedback. But keep in mind that everyone is assaulted with emails, and you are lucky if they won't discard yours in under three seconds if it is email #508 of the day.

That's why every single follow-up correspondence to a prospective client should be in your own handwriting, accompanied by a stamp.

By doing this single action, your odds of having it actually seen by a pair of eyes rocket into the next orbit.

If you have a presentation coming up, invite them to attend.

If you are asked to moderate a panel at a conference, see if they will agree to serve on it with you. It's great exposure for them, and a perfect opportunity to work closely together and showcase your talents.

If you write an article, share it, and state in the letter, "I thought it might be of interest to you."

Eventually, one of two things are going to occur:

(1) A cease and desist letter (or they will just tell you to stop bothering them)

(2) Or you wear them down enough that they finally wave the white flag and hand you the business.

About a year later, I was paired in a golf foursome at a summer conference with the vice president of Claims from a small-town insurance company. We were in the same cart for over five hours.

There is no better way to get to know a person than by wading through 18 holes on a golf course. With ample time to talk, I learned about where he grew up, his wife, kids, hobbies, and his passion for golf. I discovered that we both rose up fast in our professions and possessed similar goals. We totally hit it off.

Six months later, I learned that the manager who I bought the book for was retiring. The company was hiring a new litigation manager. The VP of Claims put in a good word for us, and after three years of dogged pursuit, we received our first assignment.

As the late, great basketball coach Jimmy Valvano once stated: "Don't give up … don't ever give up."

Chapter 9: How to Generate Clients through Speaking

"A good speech should be like a woman's skirt; long enough to cover the subject and short enough to create interest." --- Winston Churchill

If you were visiting the zoo, and a lion somehow got loose on the grounds, would you be able to look away?

Rest assured, you would be watching that animal's every move. You would be captivated. Mesmerized.

That's the same reaction you want from your audiences as a public speaker from the moment you step on stage.

In order to do that, you must undertake incredible preparation well in advance. Write out your speech. Be descriptive in terms of time, place, smells, sounds, and tastes.

Rewrite, rewrite, and rewrite.

Then memorize that story until you know it by heart. Practice it in the car on your way to work, or when you are in the midst of a morning run. Soon, it will become part of your DNA.

Once you have that part nailed down, decide how you are going to incorporate voice variations and body language to bring the story to life. Figure out the moments when you should raise or lower your voice. When is a good time to pause? Determine when you move, how you move, and the precise spots where you will land on stage.

This is a lonely, exhausting, pain-staking process. But it is the price to pay for greatness.

Most people aren't willing to make the sacrifice. That is why they suck on stage. Is there anything worse than a horrible, unprepared speaker?

I wanted to be a dynamic speaker on stage, so I soaked up everything I possibly could from my mentor, Bo Eason (www.boeason.com), inarguably the greatest public speaker I have ever seen. If you want to be the best, you have to go where the best are on stage. That is why I have endured numerous cross-country trips to California.

While Bo is a terrific storyteller, what makes him so electrifying on stage is his ability to use his body as a form of expression to bring the story to life. You literally can't take your eyes off him. The way he describes a preseason NFL practice involving Joe Montana, Jerry Rice and the other receivers makes you feel as if you were right there with him.

ACTIONABLE TIPS

The biggest thing Bo has taught me is that **the first seven seconds of your speech is the most important time frame.** The audience is going to decide right then and there whether they are coming along with you for the ride, or prefer checking their email.

There is no better way to immediately grab them than by telling a gripping personal story. Open yourself up to the audience. Be vulnerable. It's OK. The audience is on your side. They love hearing great stories.

Maybe you overcame cancer. Perhaps you survived a plane crash, or a near-death experience. The story you tell doesn't have to be incredible. Michael Jordan's fuel for his greatness was getting cut from his basketball team in high school.

You simply have to step back, examine your life, and decide the right story to share. It will become the launching pad for your success.

For 23 years, I buried that story about my fraternity. It was too embarrassing and painful to discuss. Bo taught me that it was okay to share those difficult times with the rest of the world, because it represented a defining moment in my life, and provided the springboard for my success.

Reliving painful times is never easy, but once you have that audience in the palm of your hand, it is a seamless transition to the real reason you are there: to teach.

Whatever topic you have been hired to speak on, provide them value that no one else can match. Flesh out your key points through stories. They bring the concepts to life.

Depending upon the venue, you might not be able to "pitch" your product at the end. If you can, precisely lay out **how the audience can spend more time learning from you well after your speech.** They will want more of you.

Demonstrate how their lives will transform, and how they can't afford to miss out on this opportunity. Create a scarcity. Put the audience into a time crunch.

If you are that good up on stage, people will be lining up to meet you once you walk off the stage, and flocking to do business with you.

"We are all storytellers. We all live in a network of stories. There isn't a stronger connection between people than storytelling."

— Jimmy Neil Smith

Chapter 10: Dazzle, and Earn Repeat Business and Referrals

"Exceed your customer's expectations. If you do, they'll come back over and over. Give them what they want – and a little more." --- Sam Walton

When was the last time someone blew you away?

I was on a week vacation with my wife in Lexington, Kentucky, without the kids. Total relaxation.

Bourbon. Horses. Massages. Golf. More bourbon. There is bourbon in everything down there.

Night one, a bottle of champagne shows up in the hotel room.

Night two, chocolate strawberries and cookies are delivered.

Night three, a $100 dinner certificate arrives.

Does your boss ever do this for you? Mine did.

I told everyone this story. Family. Friends. Neighbors. Guys in my tennis league. The lady that cuts my hair. Funny … none of their bosses did anything like that.

Just a hunch: I assume you would want to come back on a daily basis and work for my boss.

The same rationale can be applied when you finally land that coveted client. Don't just do a good job on that first business deal. Find a way to continually surprise them, rock their world, provide them more value than they have any right to expect, and routinely leave them breathless.

Do that, and you won't need to say a word. Your clients will become your most ardent ground soldiers, advocates, and business feeders. They will make every possible attempt to let the planet know about your superstar powers. Word-of-mouth is the most potent marketing on the planet.

W. Edwards Deming once said, "Profit in business comes from repeat customers; customers that boast about your product and service, and that bring friends with them."

I was once sent to Indianapolis to assist with expanding our business with a current client, an insurance company for our firm's offices in Indiana. We were packed like sardines into a small room.

I learned that the litigation manager who doled out the work had just celebrated her 20th year with that insurance company.

"So, what do they give you for being here 20 years?" I asked.

She replied: "Nothing."

When I got back to Michigan, I sent her the world's largest birthday card from a company called sendoutcards.com. It read: "Since your company won't recognize you for 20 years, we will. Congratulations from our law firm."

We also included a nicely wrapped box with a red ribbon on top, which was stacked with a dozen of the most delicious chocolate chip brownies on this earth.

I received a new assignment from that client the next week, and I was there simply to pitch Indiana.

I guess that's one way to leave an indelible impression.

For sake of clarity, you don't need to break the bank and continually flood your clients with gifts. But the occasional surprise doesn't hurt your standing.

In the end, retaining clients usually comes down to the little things, like attention to detail. Find out if they generally prefer to communicate by email, or phone. Return all phone calls within 24 hours. They are calling you for a reason. If you are buried in work, or mired in endless meetings, send them a quick message to advise that you are tied up, but will call them back at a certain time.

Is there anything more frustrating when someone does not call you back for three days?

Everyone pretends as if they are important, that their life is one big parade of events. In reality, nobody is that busy. Ever.

To change things up, throw a curveball. Call clients for reasons that have NOTHING to do with business.

Maybe their blossoming teenager was competing in a state golf tournament over the weekend, and you were curious how that panned out. Will we be seeing him one day at the Masters?

Or perhaps you were intrigued to hear how that all-inclusive vacation to Mexico went, and whether you should book the same resort down the road. (I actually did that. Go to the Dominican Republic in May. The resorts are empty, and half the price.)

These calls show that you actually listened when they spoke, and demonstrate you truly care about something else other than the bottom line. It will mean the world to the clients, and separate you from the competition.

I also routinely encourage my clients to call me up when they are caught in a bind. We call it the "you-can-quickly-pick-my-brain-for-free" assistance. This is the off-the-clock, no-charge scenario which certain people like to take advantage of more than others.

Let's be real. Nobody likes to work for free. Yet, that instant access to your five minutes of genius when they are in a pinch goes a long way. Clients won't forget that, particularly when that problem begins to spiral out of control, and there is a three-alarm fire raging. You will be the first one they call, because you were there for them when it counted.

ACTIONABLE TIPS

Here are some other ideas you can implement in your business to continually WOW your clients. A lot of this goes back to when you developed that personal relationship, and found out about their hobbies and passions:

- One of my clients is heavily into fitness and eating right. I sent him an email with a podcast from one of the leading gurus on plant-based diets. (I had no idea that the same person's book was sitting on his nightstand!)
- Find out if they support any charities. Show up at an event they are involved in (which align with your causes), or make a donation.
- Does your client have a favorite author? Buy one of the books, have

it signed by the author, and send it to him/her.
- One of my clients is a huge Notre Dame fan. As you know, I am a huge Michigan fan. When we first started working together, I would send her an email every Monday morning during the college football season taking a jab at Notre Dame's performance over the weekend. When I forgot to send it one Monday, she sent me an email wondering why I had not sent her one!

In the end, it is the little things you remember about your client that will not be forgotten.

Reliability, punctuality, and exceeding expectations are the cornerstones of fantastic customer service. Make it a habit to deliver greatness on a daily basis. Never take anything for granted. If you start to take the repeat customer for granted, they may end up bailing on you.

Remember, it takes 50 times the effort and finances to land a new client than it does to keep the ones you have satisfied and thirsting for more.

Download your template to wow your clients at www.bobabramson.com/companion-course.

Chapter 11: Your 90-Day Action Plan

"All change is hard at first, messy in the middle, and gorgeous in the end." --- Robin Sharma

You have the opportunity to alter the course of your business and career right now if you are ready to buy in. Imagine what that would mean that to your bottom line? Your bank account?

If this is you, it will require a change in how you operate on a daily basis. New habits are never easy to instill.

That is why you need to start small.

Make one business call a day for the first 30 days. Small changes over time will eventually lead to big results.

Then block out a half hour per day on your calendar in Month Two, and an hour per day by Month Three. During this 90-day time span, once a week, attempt to meet someone in person. Go to their offices. Make that personal connection. Develop and foster a personal relationship.

Before you arrive at the meeting, remember the three-step formula:

(1) How is my product or service going to save them costs?
(2) How is it going to increase their profit margin?
(3) How is it going to help them in the long run?

Own the meeting. Tap into their brains and desires. Level the competition. Go for broke. Ask for the business.

Track your results. Record your follow-up. There is nothing like metrics to measure your progress.

Over the next 60 days, call several publications in your industry, and volunteer to write an article. Magazines are always looking for writers. So are e-zines and other online publications. There is a massive list of websites that pay writers at https://wordingwell.com/bamidele-websites-that-pay-writers/.

Once your article comes out, share it with your current and potential clients.

This will elevate your status as an authority on that subject.

Over the next 90 days, look ahead to possible conferences you want to attend within the next year. Find out who organizes those, call them, and ask if they are looking for speakers. Conferences usually book their speakers 6-9 months ahead of time. Once you are on the stage, electrify the audience with a gripping personal story, teach them on your subject, and they will be itching to work with you.

Do all of the above, and you will see a seismic shift in your career and your bottom line.

There's an old saying that you can lead a horse to water, but you can't make them drink it.

It's now up to you to take action!

"There are risks and costs to action. But they are far less than the long range risks of comfortable inaction."

— John F. Kennedy

Chapter 12: Author's Note + Book Recommendations

I would like to hear your success stories. What have you done to WOW your clients?

Email them to me at
bob@bobabramson.com

If you enjoyed this book, I would love if you could leave a review on Amazon.com. Maybe mention some of your favorite parts, quotes, or lessons from the book:

https://www.amazon.com/review/create-review?asin=1599891913#

Keep reading for my recommendations on dynamite books on business and public speaking...

Bob's Book Recommendations for Business and Public Speaking

The Five Levels of Leadership by John Maxwell

Turn Your Ship Around! by David Marquest

Get Clients Today by Christian Mickelson

The *War of Art* by Steven Pressfield

The Leader Who Had No Title by Robin Sharma

The Go-Giver by Bob Burg

Steal the Show by Michael Port

The Wealthy Speaker 2.0 by Jane Atkinson

Profit First by Mike Michalowicz

Will it Fly? by Pat Flynn

To obtain any of these books, visit:

http://www.bobabramson.com/recommended reading

Chapter 13: About the Author

Bob Abramson is an award-winning journalist, law firm partner, master storyteller, a dynamic public speaker, and business coach.

In his senior year of high school, Bob won five Detroit Free Press writing awards for journalism.

At age 21, his byline appeared on the front page of USA Today's Sports Section.

He has also written for Gannett News Service, the Ann Arbor News, the Lansing State Journal, the Wolverine Magazine, and the Marietta Times (Ohio). Bob was voted the top investigative sports reporter in the State of Ohio for his newspaper division by the Associated Press.

In 1998, he co-authored a book on Michigan football's 1997 national championship run, which sold 15,000 copies. Former University of Michigan head football coach Lloyd Carr said this about the book: "This is truly a wonderful book that recaptures the love and spirit of the 1997 Michigan team."

You can buy this book on Amazon. It is called *University of Michigan, 1997 National Champions.*

https://www.amazon.com/University-Michigan-1997-National-Champions/dp/B003ZKFWTG/ref=sr_1_1?ie=UTF8&qid=1481466392&sr=8-1&keywords=University+of+Michigan+1997+national+champions

Bob is a 1995 graduate of the University of Michigan, and received his law degree from University of Detroit Mercy in 2005. He is a partner at the law firm of Kopka, Pinkus, Dolin. www.kopkalaw.com

In his spare time, Bob is an avid USTA tennis player. He lives in Michigan with his wife, Alyson, and their two wonderful children.

Bob dedicates this book to his ninth-grade English teacher at Cranbrook, who taught him how to write.

Website: www.bobabramson.com

E-mail: bob@bobabramson.com

Chapter 14: Book Bob to Speak at Your Next Event

Looking for a dynamic speaker at your next event? Bob delivers entertaining keynote speeches, seminars, and workshops that are packed with an insane amount of value.

Bob has been trained by one of the top public speakers in the country, Bo Eason. Bob is a member of Toastmasters International, and part of the Toastmasters D28 Speakers Bureau.

Bob's clients include corporations and business professionals. He teaches them how to wow their clients and light a fire in their business. He also trains them to become electrifying public speakers.

If you have an upcoming speech or presentation, and have no idea where to start, you might be interested in "*The Art of Storytelling and How You Can Use Your Own Personal Story to Light a Fire in Your Business*." Here Bob teaches the three critical elements of storytelling: (1) conflict; (2) the journey; (3) the resolution.

In this interactive workshop, you will unearth your own riveting personal story, and learn how to grab an audience's attention from the first words out of your mouth.

Bob's powerful keynote,"*Light a Fire in Your Business*," is tailored to those companies who want to train their up-and-coming sales associates the inside secrets of how to land and retain clients.

Bob has brought in over a million dollars of business to his law firm, and teaches the three-part formula to become a dynamite business producer: (1) marinate; (2) go for broke; (3) dazzle.

Check out Bob in action on the stage at:

http://www.bobabramson.com/hire-bob-to-speak

Click below to see what people are saying after seeing Bob live:

http://www.bobabramson.com/testimonials/

To book Bob as a speaker, e-mail him at: bob@bobabramson.com

Chapter 15: Free Bonuses

25 TIPS TO LIGHT A FIRE IN YOUR BUSINESS

BUSINESS SELF-ASSESSMENT PLAN

PROSPECT FOLLOW-UP TRACKER

WOW YOUR CLIENTS TEMPLATE

To get a copy of these free bonuses, visit

www.bobabramson.com/companion-course

Made in the USA
Charleston, SC
19 December 2016